YEAR 5

Myths, Legends and Traditional Stories

ANN WEBLEY

Teachers' Resource for Guided Reading

A & C Black • London

Contents

Introduction   3

How to Use This Book   4

Year 5 Target Statements for Reading   5

The Path of Finn McCool

   Lesson Plans and Activity Sheets   7

The Barber's Clever Wife

   Lesson Plans and Activity Sheets   19

Taliesin

   Lesson Plans and Activity Sheets   31

Record card template   42

Author Studies   43

White Wolves Series Consultant: Sue Ellis, Centre for Literacy in Primary Education

Reprinted 2006
First published 2004 by
A & C Black Publishers Ltd
38 Soho Square, London, W1D 3HB
www.acblack.com

Text copyright © 2004 Ann Webley
Illustrations copyright © 2004 Dee Shulman, Katja Bandlow and David Wyatt

The right of Ann Webley to be identified as author and the rights of Dee Shulman, Katja Bandlow and David Wyatt to be identified as the illustrators of this work have been asserted by them in accordance with the Copyrights, Designs and Patents Act 1988.

ISBN 0-7136-7024-X
ISBN 978-0-7136-7024-0

A CIP catalogue for this book is available from the British Library.

A&C Black uses paper produced with elemental chlorine-free pulp, harvested from managed sustained forests.

Printed and bound in Great Britain by Caligraving Ltd, Norfolk

Introduction

What is Guided Reading?

Guided Reading is an important aspect of literacy work in the classroom and provides the opportunity for you to reinforce previous teaching from shared sessions. Since the Guided Reading group is small and the children are all of similar ability, teaching can be even more closely targeted in order to ensure understanding and progression.

Aims of Guided Reading

The ultimate aim of Guided Reading at Key Stage 2 is to help the children read independently. This means not only reading accurately and with expression, but being able to read beyond the simple meaning of the words in order to infer, deduce, justify and evaluate. These aspects of reading comprehension need to be taught and, therefore, you play a crucial role in choosing good quality, challenging texts and in guiding sessions at the correct pace.

How to organise Guided Reading

In planning this Guide, it has been assumed that each group has one session of Guided Reading a week. This should take place outside the Literacy Hour to ensure that you can concentrate fully on the group. Other children in the class may be doing a variety of activities depending upon age and/or ability, for example:

- working on an activity based on the previous Guided Reading session.
- reading on independently in order to prepare for discussion in the next session.
- reading a book of their own choice.

- making a personal response in a Reading Journal.
- working with a Teacher Assistant to reinforce work done during a Guided Reading session and to have extra reading practice.

These might be set up in a timetable that the children become very familiar with, thus ensuring an immediate start and full use of time.

Record keeping

You should briefly fill in notes related to each session in order to inform progression against group and individual targets. A verbatim account is certainly not needed. Instead, it is useful to note children who do not achieve targets or who exceed them in any way.

Reading Journals

Children could begin to keep a Reading Journal. They can complete any written work based on their Guided Reading book or the Class Book in this journal. As they become used to using it, they should be encouraged to make additional personal responses to what they read: this might be books read at school or at home. Some teachers find it useful to provide children with a list of ideas to get them started. Personal responses ensure that children are engaging with texts and using the strategies they are being taught in Shared and Guided Reading.

How to Use This Book

Lessons

This Guide outlines five lessons to support the use of each of the three Year 5 books with a guided reading group. The books are:

- *The Path of Finn McCool* – to help less confident readers gain more independence.
- *The Barber's Clever Wife* – a traditional tale for independent readers.
- *Taliesin* – for more experienced readers.

It is important to remember that, although these lessons take into account important elements of reading at Year 5, they cannot be directed at individual children's needs on a specific word or comprehension level. It may, therefore, be necessary to make some adjustments in order to cover the specific reading objectives that a group needs to ensure progress.

Activity Sheets

Activity Sheets are included for follow-up work either in school or at home for homework. Children should also be encouraged to write independently in a Reading Journal (see p. 3).

Lesson duration

The lessons have been planned to be around 20–30 minutes in length but could be amended to suit an individual school's timetables.

Each session should be a mix of reading aloud, reading independently and a discussion about the text. The actual amounts of time spent on each will depend on the independence of the children. Experienced readers should spend most of their time on higher order reading skills, for example prediction, inference and deduction. They may read or re-read certain sections during the session in order to support this work.

Less-experienced readers will need to spend more time each session reading aloud and you will be checking for pronunciation, phrasing and understanding of unfamiliar words. Although there are some suggestions in lesson plans for this part of the session, it is expected that you will make greatest adaptations here because you will need to focus directly on your knowledge of the needs of the group. When helping children over difficulties, you should reinforce the method you are using:

- phonics – the sound of the word.
- graphic – the look of the word.
- semantic – the meaning of the word – can this be guessed by reading on?
- contextual – the context in which the story is set.

In this way, children will get used to using these methods and this will help them towards independence. Other means of developing higher order reading skills will emerge through focussed discussion in other parts of each session.

Target Statements for Reading

The NLS target statements for reading at Year 5 will help you focus on the different elements necessary for progression in reading.

Word recognition and phonic knowledge
- Use knowledge of word, roots, derivations and spelling patterens to read unknown words.

Grammatical awareness
- Understand how complex sentences are constructed and punctuated and use this to deepen understanding when reading.

Use of context
- Understand how stories may vary, e.g. in pace, build up, sequence, complication and resolution.

Knowing how texts work:
- Identify features of different fiction genres, e.g. science fiction, adventure, myths, legends.

Interpretation and response: literary text
- Identify the point of view from which a story is told and respond to this, e.g. by retelling from a different point of view.
- Understand the difference between literal and figurative language, e.g. by discussing the effects of imagery in poetry and prose.
- Recognise how characters are presented in different ways and respond to this with reference to the text.
- Infer meaning with reference to text but also applying wider experience, e.g. why a character is behaving in a particular way.

Attitude
- Develop an active response to own reading, e.g. by empathising with characters, imagining events.
- Use the blurb, front cover, reviews, etc., to make informed decisions about which books to read.
- Take part in peer group discussions and be prepared to widen reading experience based on recommendation.

The Path of Finn McCool – retold by Sally Prue

About the book

This is an entertaining myth which explains the origin of the Giant's Causeway between Ireland and Scotland which comprises over 40,000 stones packed together and resembles stepping stones from the cliffs to the sea. Stories tell how the Causeway was created using a pick-axe by the giant, Finn McCool. During the Spring Term in Year 5, children learn that myths or folk tales contain evidence of the places in which they are set. Activity sheet 5 is related to this. However, you may prefer to use an atlas and find the places as the children meet them each lesson. The dialogue has the lyrical quality of the Irish tongue and children might be helped in their understanding of this by hearing an Irish audio tape or listening to someone with an Irish accent read part of the story.

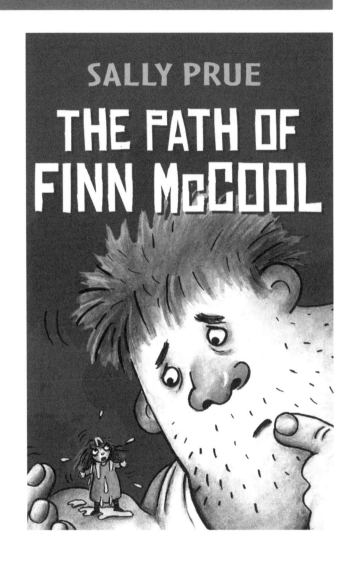

the food tent to find some ice cream and some fairy cakes.

But up on the hill, Finn McCool kept on with his hopping and hopping. He jumped and thumped and shook the ground so hard that the tent pegs juddered their way loose and the whole tent came down on the little people's heads.

Well, the little people crawled out of the tent, all rumpled and squashed, with bits of ice cream sticking out of

28

29

The Path of Finn McCool: Lesson 1

Summary of Chapter One – The start

Chapter One begins by asking the reader whether they had ever wondered about the Giant's Causeway and thus introduces the tone of traditional storytelling. Finn McCool has been told to stay away from a dance to which the little people have invited their friends from Scotland because he is so clumsy. He is upset and stands on the hill and begins to dance by himself.

Lesson plan

Introduction

Look at the front and back cover and read the blurb. Ask the children:

- What kind of story do you think it will be? What are you expecting?
- What do you know about giants?
- What sort of character is Finn?
- Does the style of illustration on the cover suggest what the tone of the story will be?

Reading and discussion

The children should take it in turns to read Chapter One aloud from their own copies of the book. Stop them to ask specific questions:

1) What picture does the image "as snug as a honeycomb" give? (p. 15). How does it help the reader understand how the stones were fitted together?

2) What evidence is there that this is an Irish story? Demonstrate reading certain sentences to show the children the lyrical quality of the writing and Irish dialect. Ask them to re-read from their own copies to show they have taken note of phrasing and the use of punctuation.

For example:

- "a great wide path of stones, it is" in the first sentence (p. 15).
- "now you'll be wondering" (p. 15).
- "terrible big, boasting fellow"(p. 17).

- "little people" – do the children understand who these are? (p. 17).
- "in a fine mood" (p. 22).

3) Can the children see any evidence that this is written as a traditional story which might be told aloud? They might identify the following sentences.

- "Now, you'll be wondering ..." (p. 15).
- "Now, this giant was lucky enough to have a wife and a baby." (p. 18).
- "Well, Finn didn't like being told what to do ..." (p. 21).

The children should be able to explain that the sentences make it sound as though someone is talking. There are other examples through the book and the children could be encouraged to find them as they read.

4) What did the children find funny in the chapter? Ask them to explain why they found something funny and justify their opinion.

5) Ask the children to take turns to read aloud the section on p. 18: "Now, this giant was lucky enough ..." to "... in his whole head". Ask them what they learn about Oona. Tell them that this will be important in the story so they should remember it as they read.

NOTE: "fifty two feet six inches" will need translating for the children! – just under 25 metres.

What to do next: The children can now complete Activity Sheet 1 "Meet Finn McCool" before the next session. This gives them the opportunity to show what they have found out so far about Finn McCool.

Meet Finn McCool!

What do we know about Finn McCool from reading Chapter One? Make notes on the sheet below, using the questions to help you. You can add extra detail to the picture if it will help.

Where does he live?

What does he look like?

Describe his personality.

Who does he live with?

White Wolves
Teachers' Resource for Guided Reading Year 5
Myths, legends and traditional stories
© A & C Black 2004

The Path of Finn McCool: Lesson 2

Summary of Chapter Two – Build-up

Finn's dance shakes the tent down on the little people's heads and they are very angry. In reply to Finn's boast that as he's the biggest giant in Ireland he can do as he likes, the chief of the Scottish little people says there is a much bigger giant in his country. Finn decides to go and see and starts building a pathway. Oona suspects that he is up to something.

Lesson plan

Introduction

1) Ask the children to summarise Chapter One in two or three sentences.

2) If the children have completed Activity Sheet 1, briefly review their ideas about Finn. Ensure that they always refer to the text when giving an opinion.

Reading and discussion

The children should now read Chapter Two. They could take turns to read sections aloud in order to check expression and phrasing. In addition, give the children the opportunity to read a short section in their heads and then answer specific questions, such as the ones outlined below.

1) Read aloud the sentences which include the phrases "clod-hopping oaf" (p. 27), "hopping and bopping" (p. 28) and "jumped and thumped" (p. 28). Ask the children what they notice. They should be able to explain that the rhyme and rhythm helps the reader to picture what is going on as well as add to the description of the character.

2) Ask the children what "or he'd never hear the last of it" means? (p. 33). What does it tell the reader about Oona? (It tells that reader that Oona is quick to criticise Finn for his stupidity.)

3) Ask the children for their opinion about how Finn has behaved. Do they think he is doing the right thing? They need to explain their reasons with reference to the text.

What to do next: The children can now complete Activity Sheet 2: "This is what I think" before the next session. This focuses on the characters and asks the children to consider what they might be thinking about.

This is what I think

Write thought bubbles for the characters in Chapter Two. Look back at the story and include as much detail as you can.

What does Oona think Finn is up to?

What does Finn think of the way the little people are speaking to him?

What does the chief of the Scottish Little People think about Finn?

The Path of Finn McCool: Lesson 3

Summary of Chapter Three: Crisis

Finn continues to build the path to Scotland. Oona gets home from her sister's house to find Finn missing. Meanwhile, Finn sees the Scottish giant, Benan Donner, who is indeed bigger than him! Scared out of his wits, he runs back across his path to Ireland.

Lesson plan

Introduction
Ask the children to summarise what has happened so far by describing the action to a friend.

Reading and discussion
1) The children should take turns to read Chapter Three aloud. Stop at key points to ask the children what they think will happen next:

- When Oona hears the thunder: "There was only a sound like thunder a long way across the sea." What do they think was causing the thunder? (pp. 46-48).

- When the thunder gets much louder: "It got louder and louder, but there was no rain at all." Why didn't Finn realise that it was the giant? (p. 49).

- When the giant appeared: "And then over the hill Finn saw something coming." (p. 50).

- The end of the chapter – what will happen next?

2) Ask the children to find the simile "as snug as a honeycomb" in their copies (p. 42). Do any of them remember the repetition from the first chapter? Remind them that repetition is one of the elements of traditional storytelling.

3) Ask the children:
- Why didn't Oona do anything when she heard the thunder?
- Does she know who it is?
- Is she worried?

4) Ask the children to find the sentence which includes the clause: "the ground shivered under his feet." (p. 49). What does the verb "shiver" suggest? How does it help the reader imagine the scene?

5) Point out to the children two occasions when a comment is made about Finn which is followed by "but". Ask them to find the following two sentences in their own copies of the story:

- "Now, Finn had a big head, and inside it was mostly empty space, but that didn't mean he couldn't use a hammer." (p. 41).

- "Now, Finn had a big head, and what was inside was mostly wind, but he was out of the lake and running as fast as he could the moment Benan Donner was out of sight." (p. 54).

Discuss the meaning of the sentence and the effect of the "but". The children should comment that the first part of each sentence describes Finn's stupidity. The second part is something useful he will do. The "but" injects humour by putting them in stark contrast.

> **What to do next:** The children can now consider what might happen next by completing Activity Sheet 3: "What happens next?" before the next lesson.

What happens next?

Can you make predictions about what will happen after Chapter Three?

What do you think Finn will do next?

What do you think Benan Donner will do next?

What do you think Oona will do next?

What would *you* do if you were Finn?

What would *you* do if you were Benan Donner?

What would *you* do if you were Oona?

White Wolves
Teachers' Resource for Guided Reading Year 5
Myths, legends and traditional stories
© A & C Black 2004

The Path of Finn McCool: Lesson 4

Summary of Chapter Four: Complication

Finn arrives home and tells Oona what has happened and that the giant will be able to follow him across the path. Oona starts to plan. She puts an iron griddle in the middle of a cake before it goes into the oven and makes Finn dress up and get into the baby's cradle. The giant arrives at their house and breaks down the door.

Lesson plan

Introduction
Ask the children to talk to a partner and tell each other in one minute what has happened in the story so far.

Reading and discussion
1) The children should take turns to read sections from Chapter Four aloud (such as p. 61 from "Finn McCool didn't stop running ..." until "griddle she used when she made scones" on p. 64 and then from "The thunder was getting closer ..." to "'... Benan Donner is coming up the path'" on pp. 67-69).

2) Ask the children:
- Why has Oona put the griddle in the cake? Explain that a griddle is a kind of iron sieve or grill.
- Why has Oona put Finn in the baby's cradle? Do the children think the plan will work?

3) Ask the children to find the following two sentences in their copy of the text.
- "You've forgotten about your secret weapon." (p. 66).
- "Have I got a secret weapon" he asked hopefully. (p. 66).

4) Discuss with the children what they think this weapon is. (This will be revealed at the end of the story.) Have they remembered about Oona's brains? What does the word "hopefully" tell the reader about Finn?

> **What to do next:** Before the next Guided Reading session, the children should read to the end of the book.
>
> In addition, they can complete Activity Sheet 4: "A giant life" which relates to all the references to giants and their very large possessions. This could equally well be completed after the story is finished
>
> If you plan to carry out the drama activity suggested in Lesson 5, you may want to tell certain children which part they will be playing so that they can prepare for it.

A giant life

Finn's baby has a "rattle made out of the rib-cage of an ox". This tells us that the giants' world is MUCH bigger than our own. Find three more examples that show how big everything is. Write the sentences or phrases below.

_____

_____

_____

_____

_____

_____

Now make up some larger-than-life comparisons of your own in the spaces below. Draw a picture underneath them.

A beard as long as a … _____

_____

_____

A cradle as large as a … _____

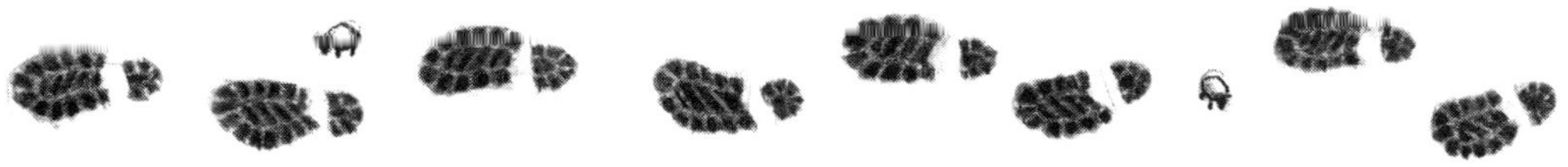

_____

_____

White Wolves
Teachers' Resource for Guided Reading Year 5
Myths, legends and traditional stories
© A & C Black 2004

The Path of Finn McCool: Lesson 5

Summary of Chapter Five – Resolution

Benan Donner enters the house. Oona gives him the cake with the griddle inside and acts surprised when he finds it so hard. She tells him that the very large "baby" takes after his father. It is now the Scottish giant's turn to be scared and he rushes back to Scotland, pulling up the stones as he goes, thus creating the causeway which is partly visible and partly under the sea.

Lesson plan

Discussion

The teacher could check understanding of Chapter Five by asking some or all of the questions outlined below.

1) Recap what the plan was and ask the children whether it worked.

2) What was the "secret weapon"?

3) Ask some of the children to re-read certain sections aloud to focus on the expression of the characters – for example the conversation between Oona and Benan Donner (pp. 75-77). Check that the children realise how Oona would have spoken.

4) Make sure the children spot more examples of Irish language:

- "Sure, and he takes after his father." (p. 83).
- "And, sure as I'm telling you." (p. 88).

Drama activity

Give the children short scenes to improvise from different points of the book in order to show what happened and the reactions and character of Finn, Oona and Benan Donner.

Examples of scenes:

- Finn and Oona at home, when Finn confesses that he's built the path which the giant will be able to cross. (pp. 61-64).
- When Oona gives the cake to Benan Donner and to Finn dressed as a baby. (pp. 76-84).

The end

1) Did any of the children spot "Now Benan Donner's big head was mostly full of air ..." on p. 83? What does it remind them of earlier in the story?

2) Discuss the fact that the last paragraph echoes back to the first section of Chapter One (p. 13). The storyteller is explaining to the reader what the story is all about.

3) How does this myth answer the question "How was the Giant's Causeway built?"

What to do next: The children can now complete Activity Sheet 5 "Ireland and Scotland" which looks at the evidence that the myth is set in Scotland and Ireland. The children might find an atlas useful. Don't forget to remind the children to fill in the key.

They might also enjoy reading other myths which are set in other parts of the world, such as the Dreamtime myths of the Aborigine people or the Scandinavian myths. Ask the children to work out what question the myth is answering.

Ireland and Scotland

This myth is set in both Ireland and Scotland. Look through the story and find names of places, islands and living creatures. Look for descriptions of the landscape and the weather.

• Write the names and phrases you find in the text on to the maps.
• Draw symbols to show animals, landmarks and other features.

Key to symbols

The Barber's Clever Wife by Narinder Dhami

About the book

The Barber's Clever Wife is a retelling of an Indian legend from the Punjab and is a classic example of a "brains over brawn" story. It contains a great deal of detail about the countryside. The first chapter is an especially rich source for this and the related Activity Sheet asks the children to find the evidence and write it around a map of India. This could be added to as the story is read.

the prisoner." He glanced over at the bunched-up quilt. "That way, I can be sure she won't escape."

The other thieves stretched out under the banyan tree, and were asleep within minutes. Peering down from the tree at the robber captain below her, Ruby wondered how she could escape.

She stared down at Karan. He looked very vain with that long, curly, black moustache. Ruby remembered how, earlier, Karan hadn't wanted to take the chance of getting his nose tip cut off.

He obviously thought a great deal of himself – and that gave her an idea. Drawing her scarf across her face, she

82

began to sing sweetly.

Startled, Karan glanced upwards. Immediately he spotted the veiled figure in the tree.

"No woman from the village would be out alone at this time of night," he muttered. "It must be a fairy spirit.

83

The Barber's Clever Wife: Lesson 1

Summary of Chapter One – Ruby starts to plan

Bulbul, a lazy barber, is sent by his wife, Ruby, to beg outside the palace. Ruby is at first furious that he is given a piece of waste land outside the city walls instead of a bullock or some useful piece of machinery. However, she says that she will think of a plan to make money from it.

Lesson plan

Introduction

Look at the front and back cover and read the blurb. Ask the children:

- What kind of story do they think it will be? What do the words "Many years ago …" in the blurb suggest?
- What might be in the jar on the cover picture? Why is someone hiding in the tree?

Reading and discussion

1) The children should take it in turns to read the first few paragraphs of the chapter aloud from their own copies so that the teacher can check the reading of long, complex sentences.

2) The children should then read on silently.

Drama activity

Look at the conversation between Ruby and Bulbul which begin on p. 11: "We simply can't go on like this," she said. Ask the children:

- What Bulbul and Ruby would say to explain their own behaviour?
- What do they think about each other's behaviour?

Ask the children to assume the roles and use evidence from the story to back up what they say. They should be able to show the contrast between the characters:

- Ruby would say that Bulbul was lazy and was content to leave things as they were. She is the one who always has to do the work! She feels irritated that her husband does not make more effort. She did not expect him to bring back much from the palace but was still annoyed that he had been given a piece of land rather than a jewel or money.

- Bulbul prefers a quiet life so he does not like it when Ruby keeps demanding that he does things. However, he is a bit scared of her and so he does as he is told. He would admit that she sent him off for a good reason. He feels really pleased with himself when he is given the land and is convinced he will never have to work again now he realises how easy it is to beg! He cannot understand why Ruby is annoyed with him.

> **What to do next:** The children can fill in Activity Sheet 1 "Out of India" before the next session. It links what they know about India already with the evidence from this first chapter.

Out of India

Write down some names of Indian people:

Write down the names of some Indian foods:

Write down some names of Indian places:

Now look back at Chapter One and write any words or phrases that show this story is set in India.

_____

_____

_____

_____

_____

_____

_____

_____

_____

_____

_____

_____

The Barber's Clever Wife: Lesson 2

Summary of Chapter Two – The first trick

The next morning Ruby puts a plan into action. She and Bulbul walk up and down gazing at the land but stop every time someone appears. This intrigues Karan, the leader of a band of thieves, and when he learns from Ruby that gold is buried on the land he goes to dig it up that night – but, of course, he finds nothing! When Bulbul and Ruby return the next day they plant seeds and in time have a successful harvest. They now have some gold. The thieves eventually realise what has happened and demand the gold for themselves. Karan insists that Mohan, one of the thieves, must steal the gold from the couple.

Lesson plan

Introduction

Ask the children to summarise what has happened so far as briefly as possible.

Reading and discussion

1) Children should take it in turns to read aloud from their own copies of the book up to "'We're waiting for someone?" Bulbul repeated. "Who?"' (p. 30). Discuss what Ruby's plan might be.

2) Ask the children to read silently to "The thieves made their living by robbing travellers, and stealing anything they could lay their hands on." (p. 32). Why might the thieves be interested in them?

3) Ask one child to read the first full paragraph on p. 33 aloud. Why did Ruby smile to herself? Have the children worked out how Ruby might be planning to use them? The word "smiled" at the end of the paragraph implies that she recognises that her plan is working.

4) Ask the children to read silently to "'That's what *you* think!" Mohan muttered to himself.' (p. 37) and then ask these questions about this section of the story.

- Confirm what Ruby's plan was. Notice how the clues are given in the text. (Ruby agrees to let Mohan help her the next day.)

- Why did Ruby lower her voice when she spoke to Mohan, one of the thieves? How would this help her plan? (She confirms that she has something important to say. By mentioning that the thieves must not hear, she gets their interest.)

- What does Mohan's comment on p.37 "That's what *you* think!" imply? (That the gold won't be there because the thieves will steal it.)

- Did the children notice evidence of Bulbul's stupidity in this section. "We are?" (p. 36) and "Why didn't you mention your grandfather's gold before?" (p. 37).

Vocabulary check

Notorious (p. 32): Demonstrate how to read on and work out the meaning from the context. Look for words that describe the thieves' behaviour and reputation: "robbing", "stealing", "hated". Check with a dictionary.

> **What to do next:** The children should read to the end of the chapter before the next session. They can now complete Activity Sheet 2: "Thick as thieves" which is about the characters' thoughts.

Thick as thieves

What might the thieves be thinking as they help Ruby dig the earth? Try to quote from the text if you can.

_____

_____

_____

_____

_____

_____

What is Ruby's opinion of the thieves? Give evidence from the text.

_____

_____

_____

_____

_____

What does Bulbul think of the thieves?

_____

_____

_____

_____

Summary of Chapter Three – Two more tricks

Bulbul finally understands that Ruby made use of the thieves and he is very nervous. Mohan tries on two occasions to steal the gold but Ruby outwits him. Karan says that he will have revenge.

Lesson plan

Introduction

Ask the children to turn to a partner and tell each other in one minute what has happened so far.

Reading and discussion

1) Ask the children to read Chapter Three silently to "… as he and his wife prepared for bed later that evening."(p. 51). Ask the children how Bulbul feels when he realises Ruby has tricked the thieves. Link the fact that he is scared now with the evidence of his character that has been discussed before. He is not one to take any risks.

2) Tell them to read on in their heads to "No one will guess where it is." (p. 52). Discuss what Ruby might be planning this time. Ensure the children know what sweetmeats are – small fancy cakes.

3) Ask the children to find the image "a thin sliver of crescent moon" on p. 53 of their copies of the book. How does this help to create the image. There is only a little light and the thief was finding it hard to see.

4) Tell the children to read on to "I'm not going to let a simple village woman get the better of me!" (p. 56). Discuss what happened and how Ruby had tricked the robbers again.

Debate

Let the children debate whether the incident on p. 55 was Mohan's fault. Karan is hostile towards Mohan for being tricked again. Mohan is defensive because he thinks his difficult mission has been a success.

Ask half the group to "play" Karan and the other half to "play" Mohan. Encourage them to use evidence from the story to back up their point of view. For example: "You idiot!" Karan roared, grabbing Mohan by the neck. "That woman's fooled you again!"

What to do next: The children should read to the end of the chapter before the next lesson. They can use Activity Sheet 3 "Whose fault is it?" as a basis for recording some of the ideas from the debate.

Whose fault is it?

On p. 55, Karan and Mohan argue about whose fault it is that Ruby foiled their plans once again. Use the spaces below to write down evidence from the story – what the characters say and do.

Karan

Mohan

The Barber's Clever Wife: Lesson 4

Summary of Chapter Four – Crisis

The thieves return at night one month later. Raju creeps into the house and Ruby – who only means to frighten him – slices off the end of his nose with her husband's razor! The same thing happens to the others except Karan who decides to give up before he gets hurt as well! Ruby puts the nose tips in a box and believes that the robbers are now bound to go away for good. But she is wrong. That night the thieves arrive when she is asleep and carry her off in her bed.

Lesson plan

Introduction

Re-cap events from the end of Chapter Three.

1) Ask the children what the three tricks have been up to the start of Chapter Four.

- Making the thieves dig a hole, only to find nothing inside it (pp. 38-40).
- Letting the thieves find the money pot which contained only vegetable peelings. (pp. 53-55).
- Letting the thieves find the bag in the mango tree filled with hornets (pp. 58-60).

2) Vocabulary check at the end of Chapter Three (p. 60):

- "Shinned" – to quickly climb using both the arms and legs.
- "Hornet" – a large wasp that nests in hollowed trees.

3) Pronunciation check – "viciously" and "suspiciously" – point out the spelling pattern.

Reading and discussion

1) The children should begin to read Chapter Four out loud from their own copies to "Ruby stood behind the open wooden shutters, and waited." (p. 67). Stop to ask them what they think Ruby will do.

2) The children should then read on silently to the end of the chapter.

3) Ask the children why Karan was more determined for revenge than ever before.

Vocabulary checks

- What does "swaggered" (p. 68) tell the reader about the way Raju moved? (It shows that he is confident in what he said and is showing his importance.)
- Lashed out: What did Ruby do? Did she mean to? Why did she act like that? (p. 62).
- What does "sniggered" tell you about the reaction? (It shows that Mohan thinks Raju has been stupid and he is not sympathetic that he has hurt himself). (p. 69)
- "Defiantly" – read around the word to check the context and then check with a dictionary. (p. 69).

What to do next: Before the next session, the children should read Chapter Five up to "Drawing her scarf across her face, she began to sing sweetly." (p. 82).

They can now complete Activity Sheet 4 "Describing the action" which investigates some of the adverbs used in Chapters Three and Four, and how these can be changed to other parts of speech.

Describing the action

These adverbs are used in Chapters Three and Four to describe the action more clearly. Look in your dictionary for ways of turning the adverbs into adjectives. In some cases, you can also create a noun.

ADVERB	ADJECTIVE	NOUN
SARCASTICALLY:	sarcastic	sarcasm
NOISELESSLY:		
NERVOUSLY:		
IMPATIENTLY:		
DEFIANTLY:		
TRIUMPHANTLY:		
STERNLY:		

Write sentences using the new words. The first one is done for you.

"Don't be sarcastic," Mum said crossly.

"I don't think sarcasm helps," Mrs Brown said, peering at Bill.

_____

_____

_____

_____

_____

_____

_____

_____

The Barber's Clever Wife: Lesson 5

Summary of Chapter Five – Resolution

Ruby is so scared when she awakes that she is unable to think of a plan. However, she manages to escape into the branches of a banyan tree, leaving the quilt behind so that it looks as though she is still asleep. Ruby sings to Karan from the tree and, making use of the fact that he thinks a lot of himself, tricks him into closing his eyes whereupon she bites off the end of his tongue. When the thieves go to the King to try to get the gold through law, Ruby shows him the nose tips and tells him how they broke into her house. The thieves are arrested and Bulbul is made Chief Minister by the King who explains that with such a clever wife he will never make a bad decision.

Lesson plan

Re-cap from reading

Review what the children read to prepare for the lesson. Focus on "and that gave her an idea" (p. 82). What do they think Ruby will do? How has Ruby's behaviour changed? There may be various suggestions as to what Ruby might do. However, the children should recognise that she is now scared for the first time.

Reading and discussion

1) The children should now take it in turns to read on with breaks to answer questions. For example:

- How is Ruby planning to trick Karan?
- Why did Karan fall for it?
- What does "wheedled" (p. 85) tell the reader?

Ask the children to continue to read aloud to "Let's get out of here!" (p. 87).

2) Now ask the children to read silently to the end. Ask them the following questions:

- Why does the King ask Bulbul to be the Chief Minister?
- Why doesn't he ask Ruby?
- Who will really advise the King?

- Do the children realise that Ruby will be the one making all the decisions (but that a woman could not be seen to have that role?)

Conclusion

1) Explain to the children that they are now going to write a response to the whole book. Use the prompts on Activity Sheet 5 "My personal response" and discuss how to do this. Demonstrate how to give a personal opinion and back it up with evidence from the text. For example, "I liked the description of the busy market on p. 15: 'people jostled and pushed each other, the shopkeepers shouted out their wares and people drove their cattle to sell them at a market.'"

2) Tell the children about some more traditional stories that are set in other countries which could be found in the school library. Encourage them to read further examples of the genre.

My personal response

Write your opinions of the book below. Write sentences and use evidence from the story wherever you can.

My favourite characters are	My favourite part of the story is	My favourite description is
because	because	because

Things I didn't like

TRADITIONAL STORIES

In traditional stories the good characters usually triumph in the end and the bad characters are usually punished. Is this true for *The Barber's Clever Wife*?

_____

_____

_____

_____

Did you like the ending of the story?

_____

_____

Did you think it was fair?

_____

_____

White Wolves
Teachers' Resource for Guided Reading Year 5
Myths, legends and traditional stories
© **A & C Black 2004**

Taliesin by Maggie Pearson

About the book

This is a legend based on the stories of Taliesin who was a Welsh bard in the late sixth century. In this novel Taliesin is a magician, phrophet and trickster, with the power to change the fortunes of all he encounters.

"I'm not a fisherman," protested Elphin. "I'm cousin to the King!" Though he had to admit a hundred pounds would come in handy for fixing the castle roof.

The fishermen weren't too keen on the idea either; they didn't want Elphin the Unlucky spoiling the luck of the weir, though none of them was in any hurry to try it for himself. They'd got better things to do on May Eve. Things like feasting and dancing and keeping the bonfires blazing bright to scare off the witches and hobgoblins.

There was way too much magic about on that night of the year for any sane man to want to sit by himself on a damp

10

riverbank in the dark.

"Witches?" scoffed Elphin. "Poppycock! As for hobgoblins – I wouldn't know one if I saw one. Would you?"

That settled it. They took him down to the rivermouth and showed him how to set his nets.

"Now all you have to do," they said, "is wait till morning."

There they left him.

So there he sat, through the long, cold hours of darkness. Every time the moon peeped out from behind the clouds (which wasn't often) it gave Elphin just enough light to see that his nets were still empty. Not a ripple; not a splash; nor the shimmer of a single silvery fish.

11

Taliesin: Lesson 1

Summary of Chapter One – The coming of Taliesin

A bag is washed up near a river mouth where Elphin, a cousin of the King, is fishing. As usual, he has no luck but he discovers a baby, already able to talk, inside the bag. Elphin says "Taliesin", meaning "what a bright face", when he sees the child and this becomes his name. The baby seems to know that Elphin has always wanted a son. He takes the child home to Olwen, his wife. One evening, Taliesin starts to tell the couple his story.

Lesson plan

Introduction

Look at the cover and read the blurb. What kind of story are they expecting? What can they see across the boy's face? (A Celtic pattern.) Are the children familiar with the words "trickster", "prophet" and "magician".

Reading and discussion

1) Ask one of the group to read the first paragraph aloud. Do the children have any ideas what might be in the bag?

2) Ask the children to read on to the next break in the text: "As if all his troubles until now had been nothing but one long bad dream." (p. 14). Discuss some or all of the aspects outlined below:

- Why did someone suggest that Elphin fish on May Day Eve? (Because good luck is inevitable.) Why were the others not keen to join him? (They thought Elphin might spoil the luck associated with the weir.)

- Look closely at the paragraph on p. 11 beginning "So there he sat ..." Point out the use of the semi-colons to provide balance to the sentence and the repetition which is often a part of traditional storytelling.

Discuss the vivid description, especially the personification in "a clinging mist that coiled long cold fingers round him, chilling him to the bone." (p.12).

- On p. 13, who did Elphin think might have been singing? (The fishermen enjoying the May Day Eve festivities.)

3) Ask the children to read silently to the end of the chapter and then ask the question again. They may now suggest that it was Taliesin.

4) Ask the children what is happening in the section on p. 19 beginning, "There's nothing like a new baby ..." Why do they think that Taliesin did not speak?

5) Discuss the structure of the plot and that there will now be a flashback because Taliesin has begun to tell his story to explain how he came to be with them.

What to do next: The children can now complete Activity Sheet 1: "Elphin's thoughts" which asks them to write down Elphin's thoughts at significant points in Chapter One.

Ask the children to read Chapter Two before the next session.

Elphin's thoughts

Write down what Elphin would be thinking. Use the first person:

1. When someone suggested fishing on May Day Eve.

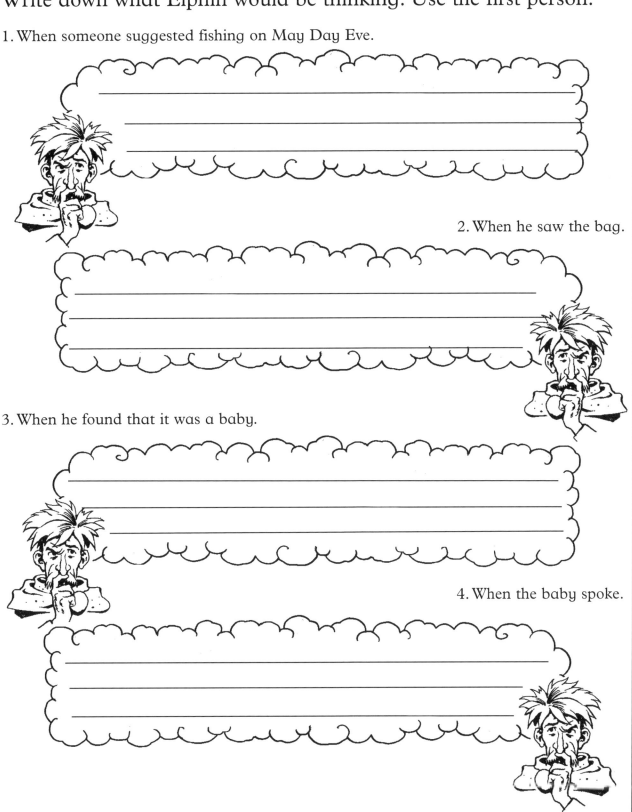

2. When he saw the bag.

3. When he found that it was a baby.

4. When the baby spoke.

White Wolves
Teachers' Resource for Guided Reading Year 5
Myths, legends and traditional stories
© **A & C Black 2004**

Taliesin: Lesson 2

Summary of Chapter Two – Taliesin's story: a flashback

Taliesin tells how a witch called Caridwen gave shelter to an old man and a boy in return for helping stir a brew which would make her all-powerful. Just before the allotted year and a day was up, the boy, Gwion, gets three drops of the liquid on his hands and is flooded with knowledge. He rushes off as the cauldron cracks and the rest of the brew is spilt. The witch gives chase, changing quickly from old woman to greyhound to otter to hawk and finally to a hen. Gwion runs off and becomes a hare, a fish, a bird and then a grain of corn. However, Caridwen, in the guise of the hen, swallows the seed and thinks she has won. In time, she gives birth to a baby. She is so afraid of his magic that she puts him in a bag and throws him in the sea. Taliesin assures the old couple that the story is the truth.

Lesson plan

Discussion about structure

1) Discuss the flashback. Ask the children if they noticed when the story in flashback catches up with the present – "'And here I am!' cried Taliesin." (p. 37).

Discuss other stories that the children have read which include flashbacks, such as Step by Wicked Step by Anne Fine, in which five children relate episodes from their own lives to each other. They may also be able to give examples from television and cinema.

2) Ask the children to find the sentence, "Elphin wrinked his nose: 'Something's burning.'" at the end of Chapter One in their own copy of the story. (p. 22). Then ask them to find the sentence "The rest of the brew boiled up and cracked the cauldron clean in two with an almighty CLANG!" in Chapter Two (p. 32).

Now discuss the following questions:
- What has happened to the brew? (It has burned because the boy has stopped stirring.)
- What did Elphin sense in Chapter One? (He sensed the burning – he could smell it.)

Ensure that the children realise that the couple have begun to "experience" Taliesin's story through magic.

Re-read and discuss

Ask the children to re-read certain passages in order to question them about all or some of the points outlined below.

1) Vocabulary check

If any of the children are unsure, demonstrate how to use the context to deduce the meaning.
- "Hemlock" – a poisonous plant with fern-like leaves and small white flowers. (p. 26).
- "Mandrake" – a poisonous and addictive plant. (p. 26).
- "Scoured" – searched thoroughly. (p. 28).
- "Stoked" – added fuel to a fire. (p. 29).

2) Effective punctuation

Point out the ellipsis on p. 29: "Stirring a foul-smelling cauldron day after day after day ..." Then read the next sentence. What does the ellipsis suggest to the reader? (That time passed and the boy continued to do that task.)

3) Ask the children if they think the brew was spilled on purpose? They should give their opinion and use evidence to back it up.

> **What to do next:** Ask the children to read Chapter Three before the next session. They can now complete Activity Sheet 2: "Magic!" which is concerned with all the magic and magical objects in Chapter Two.

Magic!

Chapter Two is full of magical objects and events. Re-read the chapter and list anything you find. Then illustrate your work.

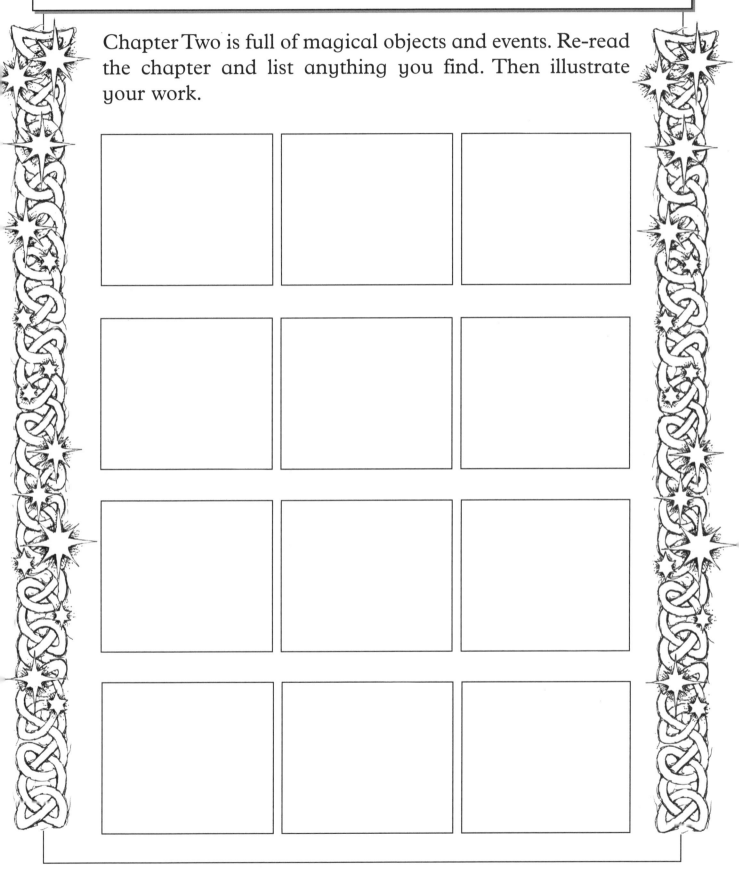

Taliesin: Lesson 3

Summary of Chapter Three: Crisis

Taliesin spends 12 years with the couple and always gives good advice. Unexpectedly, Elphin is invited to his cousin's court. He foolishly tells someone there that he hates it and that his wife is more beautiful than the King's. As a result he is thrown into the dungeon. Taliesin speaks to Elphin inside his head to reassure him. Taliesin arranges for Olwen to swap places with a peasant servant in time for a visit from the King's son, Rhun. When Rhun sees the girl, he assumes it is Elphin's wife and chops off her fat finger, while she is lying drunk, as proof. Taliesin heals the finger. Rhun returns with the finger and Elphin points out that this cannot possibly be his wife. Rhun is so furious that everyone is laughing at his mistake that he throws Elphin back in the dungeon.

Lesson plan

Introduction

Ask the children to summarise what has happened in the story so far.

Re-reading

Ask the children to silently re-read the first section to the break in the text.

1) Vocabulary check
- "Druid" – an ancient Celtic priest, magician or soothsayer (p. 41).
- "Bard" – a Celtic minstrel (p. 41).

2) Why did Taliesin "practise what he already knew"? (p. 42). (The children need to understand that he has knowledge from his former life but must grow up gradually.)

3) Why did people think that Elphin had caught the "magic salmon of wisdom".

Check if the children can make the link back to Chapter One and suggest why the villagers assumed his luck had changed. Why had his luck changed?

4) Why did Taliesin whisper in Elphin's ear? Ensure that the children understand that all the wisdom comes from the boy.

Drama activity

Ask the children to quickly re-read the next section in their heads. Hot-seat Elphin at court with either the teacher or a member of the group playing Elphin. The others should question him about his behaviour in order to gain understanding about his character.

1) Ask one of the children to read aloud the section from "Alone in his prison cell …" to "And he did have sweet dreams." (pp. 53-54).

Ensure that the children understand that Taliesin is talking to Elphin inside his head. Why does he say "Nothing I can't handle" in answer to Elphin's question, when nothing has actually happened to Olwen? Do the children understand that the wizard has the knowledge of what will come?

2) Ask the children to summarise orally what happens next. Did any of the children remember Taliesin's advice before he set off for court – that he should say that everything about the King, his family and his Kingdom is the best?

3) Ask one of the children to read the long complex sentence beginning "How they'd laugh when …" (p. 59). If necessary, demonstrate careful reading which uses expression and takes account of punctuation.

> **What to do next:** Ask the children to read Chapter Four before the next session. They can now answer questions about the chapter they have just been discussing on Activity Sheet 3 "What happens next".

What happens next?

Answer these questions using evidence from Chapter Three.

1. List the ways Elphin was now able to help his people.

_____

_____

_____

_____

2. Why did Elphin say that his wife was more beautiful than the Queen when he had been advised not to?

_____

_____

_____

_____

3. How did Taliesin trick Rhun when he visited the house?

_____

_____

_____

_____

4. How was Elphin able to prove that Rhun had made a mistake?

_____

_____

_____

_____

5. Why was Rhun so furious?

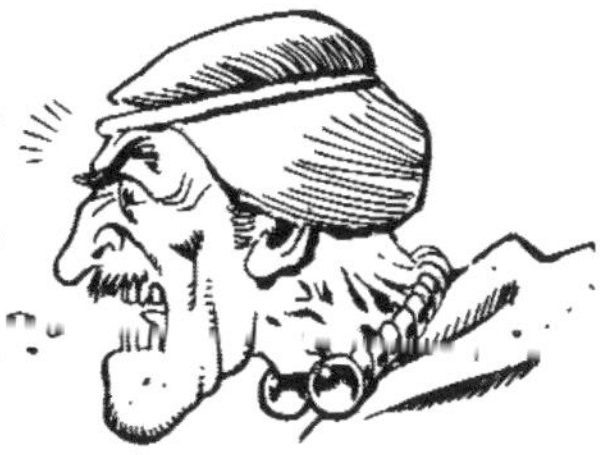

_____

_____

_____

_____

Taliesin: Lesson 4

Summary of Chapter Four – Magic at work

Taliesin and Olwen arrive at the King's court. Olwen confronts the King who agrees that she is indeed prettier than his wife. After dinner, the bards enter and Taliesin's magic results in them all making rude noises which they cannot stop. Taliesin goes before the King and claims to be the best bard. He sings a song which so impresses the King that he says Taliesin can name his reward.

Lesson plan

Re-reading

1) Ask one member of the group to re-read the first paragraph and discuss the meaning behind "I knew you'd say that." (p. 67). (Taliesin had created a situation which would mean that Olwen would get involved when it was right for her to do so.)

2) Look at the section when the bards entered the hall. Ask the children to quickly re-read from "The two of them … " to "That broke the spell". (pp. 67–73).

3) Vocabulary check

Make sure the children understand the meaning of "dignified" (p.70). (It means worthy of respect.)

4) Do the children understand that Taliesin bewitched each group as they passed him?

5) What caused the spell to break? (Heinin Vardd being cuffed on the head by Rhun.)

6) Choose one of the group to read the song aloud. Ask the children to discuss what they think it is about. (The song is about Taliesin always being in the world and being one with nature.)

7) Prediction

Ask the children what they think Taliesin will ask for.

> **What to do next:** The children should read to the end of the book before the next session. Activity Sheet 4 "What happened?" is designed for their notes as they read. This will aid discussion in the next session.

What happened?

As you read Chapter Five make notes as bullet points under the following headings.

Describe what happens ...

at the summoning of the winds

_____

_____

_____

at the horse race

_____

_____

_____

at the end

_____

_____

_____

Things I liked or found interesting

_____

_____

_____

_____

Things I want to discuss because I don't understand

_____

_____

_____

_____

Taliesin: Lesson 5

Summary of Chapter Five – The resolution

Taliesin asks for Elphin to be set free. When the King refuses, Taliesin assures him that within an hour he will be glad to free the prisoner. Taliesin sings again and summons the four winds which meet at the castle, creating havoc all the way. The King is afraid and sets Elphin free, thus proving Taliesin correct. The King suggests a horse race between Elphin's horse and the best in the King's stable. The following morning, Elphin discovers that he is racing against 24 horses. Taliesin places sprigs of holly on the ground in front of the King's horses. These cast shadows which look like a wall. The King's horses stop and Elphin wins. During the race, Elphin drops his hat. Taliesin borrows a spade and tells him to dig in that spot. Elphin finds a crock of gold as repayment for looking after the boy. Taliesin leaves, telling Elphin that he will be able to manage on his own.

Lesson plan

Discussion

Allow the discussion to link with the points that the children have made on Activity Sheet 4 – and especially anything they did not understand. Some or all of these points could be discussed.

1) What do they think the song meant?

2) Why did the King let Elphin go?

3) Ask one of the children to read the paragraph beginning "With a crash ..." (p. 83). If necessary, demonstrate reading the first sentence with expression and using the punctuation to aid understanding.

Discuss the effect of the very short sentence that follows. (It is especially effective because the long sentence describes the effect of the winds. The short sentence echoes the way the noise stopped – suddenly.)

4) Ask the children why the King did not just let Elphin go home at that point. Why did he suggest the horse race? The children may suggest different motives. If they remember what Taliesin said at the beginning about the King's horses, they may say that the King wanted to prove to Elphin that he did have something that was the best. Some may suggest he was being friendly.

The end

1) Will things change for Elphin now that Taliesin has gone? (He has the gold pieces and he has the promise that, if he closes his eyes, Taliesin will be there – the implication is to help him.)

2) You could also research some of the sources of information about the legend of Taliesin and invite the children to compare these ideas with those in the book.

Tell the children about other legends that are in the school library that they could read and enjoy.

> **What to do next:** The children can now make notes on Activity Sheet 5 "A personal response". The notes could then be used to write up a personal response to the book in their Reading Journals.

A personal response

Make notes for a personal response to this story. Think about what you enjoyed and what you did not like as much and say why. Write your notes under the following headings:

• plot

_____

_____

_____

• the opening and ending

_____

_____

_____

• characters

_____

_____

_____

• the magic

_____

_____

_____

• the setting

_____

_____

_____

• the meaning behind the story

_____

_____

_____

Record Card

Group:	Book:
Focus for session:	

Names	Comments

About the Author: Sally Prue

Sally Prue

At school, Sally Prue was intrigued by language, but she wasn't very good at creative writing. Now she is recognised as one of today's most exciting and talented new writers. All her novels have received widespread acclaim – her first, *Cold Tom*, won the Smarties Prize and the Branford Boase Award. Sally is married with two children and has lived in Hertfordshire since she was adopted as a baby. She combines writing with teaching recorder and piano. Her hobbies include painting, gardening, walking and daydreaming.

The White Wolves Interview

Where did the idea for The Path of Finn McCool come from?
The story of the Giant's Causeway has been one of my favourites since I was a child. I had a teacher called Mr Casey who was always telling us funny stories, and I expect I heard it first from him.

What's the hardest thing about writing stories – and the easiest?
I'm just an ordinary sort of person – I've never been particularly clever, or funny or brave – so the hardest thing is believing I can do it enough to start writing. The easiest bit is all the crossing-out. I really feel I'm improving it, then!

What do you enjoy doing when you're not writing?
I really like eating and sleeping and talking and reading and walking and pottering about and making things. I like playing the piano and the recorder and the bagpipes, too.

What did you enjoy reading when you were young – and what do you enjoy reading now?
I read a lot when I was young because stories were much better than real life. I loved the Narnia books, and Paddington, and later on, Ronald Welch's military books. Nowadays, I still read lots of children's books, but also quite a lot of old-fashioned stuff like Jane Austen.

About the Author: Narinder Dhami

Narinder Dhami

What's the hardest thing about writing stories – and the easiest?
The hardest thing for me is to get started – I keep putting it off! The easiest thing for me is writing dialogue. I love that part.

What do you enjoy doing when you're not writing?
I love reading. I go the gym, play with my five cats and look after my garden. I also love shopping and travelling – I've been to India twice.

What did you enjoy reading when you were young – and what do you enjoy reading now?
I used to like Enid Blyton when I was very young, then I moved on to reading anything except science-fiction (which I still don't like). Now I enjoy reading biographies, especially the lives of famous authors.

Narinder Dhami was born in Wolverhampton, to an Indian father and English mother. She always wanted to write, but trained to be a teacher instead. After ten years, she gave it up to write full-time. Luckily, the first book she wrote, *A Medal for Malina*, was accepted by the first publisher she sent it to! At first she wrote exclusively for children's magazines, but now she writes novels. Many of her early books were published as parts of long-running series but she is quickly gaining a reputation as a writer of high-quality stand-alone fiction. Narinder now lives in Cambridge with her husband, Robert, and their five cats.

The White Wolves Interview

Where did the idea for The Barber's Clever Wife come from?
I know quite a lot of stories from India because my dad used to tell them to me when I was little.

About the Author: Maggie Pearson

Maggie Pearson

Since leaving university, Maggie Pearson has had a variety of jobs: librarian, barmaid, au pair, and freelance journalist, but primarily as a mother. It was only after her three sons had grown up that she decided to concentrate on writing full-time. To date, she has published over thirty books – from retellings of folk tales to teenage novels.

The White Wolves Interview

Where did the idea for Taliesin come from?
I didn't make it up! The story of Taliesin dates from the Dark Ages, though it wasn't written down till several hundred years later, which is why parts of it sound more like a fairytale. He probably was a real person: a druid, a doctor and a bard, just like the story says.

What's the hardest thing about writing stories – and the easiest?
Forcing myself to sit down and start writing each day. (Most writers will say the same.) What's the easiest thing? When the characters start saying and doing things that surprise me; that's when I know the story is "working".

What do you enjoy doing when you're not writing?
Reading, crosswords, going to the theatre and travelling abroad.

What did you enjoy reading when you were young – and what do you enjoy reading now?
There weren't many good children's books about, but my father used to make up bedtime stories for my sister and me. They were quirky, funny and ended with a cliffhanger every night. When he ran out of ideas, he used to tell us folk tales. My favourite was "The Boy who cried Wolf." These days I read all sorts of books – about three a week. My favourite children's writers are Leon Garfield, Anne Fine, Diana Wynne Jones and Lemony Snicket.

Dan is in trouble at school, but he isn't to blame. If he and Billy become detectives, can they solve the mystery together?

There's been a robbery at Doogood's furniture shop but Police Constable Penny Penrose has been ordered to count traffic cones. Still, that doesn't stop her dogs, Scratch and Sniff getting on the case. Apart from sticky buns, there's nothing they like better than a good mystery to solve...

Buffalo Bert isn't like any other grandad. He's always doing crazy things. Sunny thinks Bert is great – until she makes a new set of friends at school.

As Scott passes the basement steps of his new school, there's a bang and a crash and a roaring sound. Scott knows there's something down there... something nasty... something dangerous. What is it? Can Scott piece together the clues and solve the mystery?

Cal is helping out on Mr Jessop's stall. It's a tough job. He needs to be quick, clever and fair – especially when something valuable comes along.

There are signs of a ghost in Granpa's creaky old house. Bits of it have been left in the chimney and you can hear its heartbeat at night. So when Adam dares his brother and sister to get on the ghost trail and hunt it down in the graveyard at midnight, who will be brave enough to go with him?

This resource will help teachers use three White Wolves books for guided reading lessons in the classroom. It includes five guided reading teaching sequences plus photocopiable worksheets for each of the books.

This resource will help teachers use three White Wolves books for guided reading lessons in the classroom. It includes five guided reading teaching sequences plus photocopiable worksheets for each of the books.

White Wolves Resources for Guided Reading

Year 4

When Hugo breaks his arm, he thinks he'll be bored and useless. But with his mum's new reaching, grabbing and twirling invention, Hugo's world is turned upside down!

Luke loves visiting his grandad and helping out with the pigeons. But Grandad gets sick and muddled and needs more than Luke's help. When he goes into hospital, events take a turn for the worst and suddenly Luke has to grow up very fast...

Zoey leads an ordinary life, but her secret wishes are far from normal. One magical day, she logs on to the net and finds she has the chance to make her wildest dreams come true.

Carly is being teased and excluded from the group of girls who were once her best friends. She tries to put a brave face on it, but it's clear that she has "lost her fizz". Then Carly finds a stray dog that needs a loving home and all at once life starts looking very different...

How did Caleb turn into a creature part boy and part swan, and come to live on the Isle of Nanna? Find out in this haunting story from a prize-winning writer.

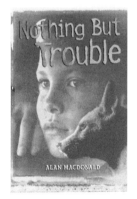

It's a tough job being Jago's "buddy" at school. The new boy comes from a family of travellers and he doesn't say much or seem interested in making friends. Then Paul discovers Jago has a secret and a special bond develops between the two boys, but how long can it last?

This resource will help teachers use three White Wolves books for guided reading lessons in the classroom. It includes five guided reading teaching sequences plus photocopiable worksheets for each of the books.

This resource will help teachers use three White Wolves books for guided reading lessons in the classroom. It includes five guided reading teaching sequences plus photocopiable worksheets for each of the books.

White Wolves Resources for Guided Reading

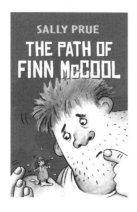

When the giant Finn McCool annoys the little people, they warn him of an even bigger giant across the sea in Scotland. Finn's big mistake is setting off to find him...

Margaret Mahy is renowned for creating vivid fantasy landscapes that enthral readers of all ages. This collection brings together five Mahy classics – by turns madcap, haunting and surreal.

Many years ago, there lived a lazy barber who lost customers by cutting them, not their hair! Luckily, he had a clever wife with cunning plans to earn the couple money...

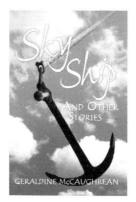

Geraldine McCaughrean has won many awards for stories set in the past. Here are five brilliant tales that will transport you to other times and places you will never forget.

A boy drinks from the magic cauldron of knowledge and is reborn as Taliesin. Now he has the power to change the fortunes of all whom he encounters – for better and for worse.

In Joan Aiken's stories, ghosts appear in both bizarre and familiar places – and none is easily forgotten. This collection of chillers is guaranteed to send a shiver down your spine.

This resource will help teachers use three White Wolves books for guided reading lessons in the classroom. It includes five guided reading teaching sequences plus photocopiable worksheets for each of the books.

This resource will help teachers use three White Wolves books for guided reading lessons in the classroom. It includes five guided reading teaching sequences plus photocopiable worksheets for each of the books.